Divorce
and the
Gospel
of Grace

Divorce
and the
Gospel
of Grace

Les Woodson

WORD BOOKS
PUBLISHER
WACO, TEXAS

DIVORCE AND THE GOSPEL OF GRACE

All Scripture quotations, unless otherwise marked, are from
the King James Version of the Bible. Quotations marked
RSV are from the Revised Standard Version of the Bible,
copyrighted 1946, 1952, © 1971, 1973 by the Division of
Christian Education of the National Council of the Churches
of Christ in the U.S.A., and are used by permission.

ISBN 0-8499-2852-4
Library of Congress Catalog Card Number 78-65808
Printed in the United States of America

Contents

Introduction 7

Part I: What Does the Bible Say? 11
           Divorce and Scripture 13
           The Heart of Jesus' Teaching 21
           How Jesus Treated the Divorced 27

Part II: What Are the Problems of the Divorced? 31
           What Would You Do? 33
           Divorce and Loneliness 40
           Divorce and Guilt 44
           Divorce and Insecurity 47

Part III: How Can the Church Minister to the
           Divorced? 51
           Structuring the Church to Deal with Divorce ..53
           The Right to Marry Again 59
           Local Church Guide to Action 64
           How to Witness to a Divorced Person 72

Notes 75

Bibliography 77

Introduction

It is known far and wide that monogamous marriage (one man and one woman living in wedlock) is being seriously threatened in our time. One aspect of this situation is the increasing prevalence of divorce. The number of divorced people in the United States has steadily climbed from 100,000 in 1914 to approximately 582,000 in 1968. One out of every three marriages in the United States today ends in divorce; it is a fair appraisal to suggest that as many as half of the married or formerly married population has been directly involved in a broken marriage.

In the face of this growing divorce rate, the church is caught up and forced to restudy its theological and ethical stance toward marriage and divorce. As the church seeks to relate itself to the dilemma of modern man, it must ask itself how it is to respond to this increasingly common situation.

For too long the church has offered no satisfactory answer to the divorced. There have been those who have ignored the biblical teachings on divorce, who have taken the flippant attitude that if man's situation makes it necessary to contradict the Word of God, then "too bad for the Bible."

More commonly, the church has taken the rigid approach that it must never remarry divorced persons or permit such remarried persons to hold office within the congregation. Dale Galloway, a clergyman whose marriage ended in an unwanted divorce, writes, "I grew up knowing how the church thought almost as well as I knew my own thoughts. Instinctively, I knew that there was no way that the people from this conservative, evangelical background would ever be able to understand my divorce. I would forever be, in their eyes, a 'second-class citizen.'"[1]

Varying shades of these extremes are to be found among religious spokesmen. It is no wonder that the divorced person often gives up on the church. In this book I have tried to take an approach that avoids either extreme, that takes the biblical teachings on divorce seriously but also offers to the divorced the hope of reconciliation through grace. This little book is written with a double compassion—compassion for the church as it confronts the mounting problem of divorce, and compassion for the divorced as they face the problems of loneliness, isolation, guilt, and rejection from the religious community.

Knowing the biblical position on sex, marriage, divorce, and remarriage is basic to any sane approach to the subject in hand. But we cannot afford to assume that people are always going to measure up. It should be apparent to all of us that men and women are bound together by the inescapable cords of human frailty and mortal imperfection. The actual and the ideal are never the same. This is why man stands in need of the gospel of grace. And it is this gospel of grace which we are seeking to understand in the following pages of this approach to divorce—Christian style.

My approach to the Bible in the following pages will be new to many readers. I have come a long way in my understanding of the Bible. My pilgrimage has taken me from fundamentalism to liberalism to conservatism to dynamism. Today, I find the Scriptures far more dynamic than what I once thought. And when I learned to read the Bible without the distorting spectacles of encrusted tradition, I found new life for me. The divine Word had suddenly become vibrant and pulsating with dynamic life-changing truth.

With my exciting discovery of the deeper intents of God's dealings with man from Adam to Christ, it is to be expected that my attitude toward the subject in this book has somewhat altered. In no way does this mean I can commend divorce. But it does mean that life is not static, and that the divorced person must be permitted to live again.

At no time has the church insisted that persons who gossip cannot be placed in positions of responsible leadership. Yet the Bible is as emphatic about gossip as a sin as it is about divorce. And the gossiping church member is never a victim of circumstances beyond his control. He does not have to hurt people with his hate-filled words. The divorced person is often caught in a dilemma which he cannot help.

Either the church must accept imperfect people for its jobs of leadership or it will accept no one at all. There is no reason for any divorced person to be a "second-class" Christian. God does not treat people like that. But we do. While we no longer stone to death those who break our idea of moral law, we often practice a mental cruelty that is a far worse sentence.

As we try to rethink our understanding of divorce and remarriage, it will be helpful if our minds are freed from stifling traditions which have been taught us from childhood. That in no way is a judgment on any particular tradition, but a call to recognize traditions for what they are—man-made receptacles in which to place truth. And Jesus warned us that the old wineskins are often so brittle as to be incapable of holding the dynamic new wine of the gospel (Matt. 9: 17).

Admittedly, none of us is ever completely free from traditions. Nor can we by an act of self-will suddenly drive out the accumulated religious conventions of a lifetime. Certainly there is every reason to hold on to any tradition which is able to breathe with the pulsating truth of the Lord Jesus Christ. But if it can no longer breathe, it is already dead and ought to be given a formal burial.

And since it is not always easy to diagnose the amount of divine life left in a tradition, we must pray fervently for the wisdom of the Holy Spirit, who promises to lead us into all truth. The following chapters will be an honest and prayerful attempt to understand the scriptural teaching on the subject, the problems of the divorced, and the role which the church can assume in relating these two concerns.

I.
What Does the
Bible Say?

Divorce
and
Scripture

While the Christian community cannot consider tampering with the commandments of God, neither can it afford to cling to traditions of man which may need rethinking. That does not mean that there is any excuse for skirting what the Word of God says. Rather, it means that we should be unafraid to check again very carefully what the scriptural references to divorce are *really* saying.

But before we can begin to wrestle seriously with what the Bible says about divorce, we must take a careful look at the biblical view of sex and marriage.

From the earliest days of Hebrew history, men have shared a rather general understanding of the origin and purpose of human sex. The story of creation suggests that God made woman because it was not good that man should be alone (Gen. 2: 18). The partner was to become his "alter ego," the other half of his life. It seems reasonable to assume that the oft-recurring sexual desire between partners is an evidence that the divine plan to obviate "aloneness" included companionship and not just procreation.

It is true that one of the more practical designs for sex was that the earth might be populated (Gen. 1: 28). All living things were to function in this fashion in order that the species might not become extinct. Man shares this necessity with the rest of the animal kingdom. It is interesting to note, however, that the human animal does not engage in sex only by instinct at mating time; human partners can be aroused to pursue each other as an act of reciprocal love. Sex was meant to bind two persons together. The fact that three persons cannot engage in the sex act at the same time is a kind of built-in suggestion that only two people belong together in this supreme giving of self to another.

Inherent in human sexuality is fidelity and trust. Only in an atmosphere of trust can sex best be used to fulfil human psychological and emotional needs as well as physical demands. For fulfilment in a relationship, two persons must deal exclusively with each other in the sexual realm. No wholesome relationship can exist in which each partner gives only a part of himself to his companion. Once the self is given, it should not be taken back to give to someone else, lest the relationship be destroyed.

The Old Testament used the Hebrew word translated into English as "know" to describe the intimacy of sexual intercourse: "Adam *knew* Eve his wife, and she conceived and bore Cain" (Gen. 4: 1, RSV, italics mine). The purpose of sex (other than procreation) was originally meant to be a sharing of one's full identity. When the sharing was a reciprocal experience, the two persons were identified as one; they became such a part of each other that any attempt at breaking up the whole would result in two halves.

From the beginning of human creation, it was God's plan that one man and one woman should form a permanent union: "Therefore shall a man leave his father and mother, and shall cleave unto his wife: and they shall be one flesh" (Gen. 2: 24). C. S. Lewis suggests that this scripture (and Jesus' reference to it in Matt. 19: 5) means that they become a "single organism." Divorce, then, is like cutting up a living body and should be done only as a last resort in marital surgery.[2]

Eve came from Adam and was given back to him as his companion; thus the two remained one flesh. Since there was no one else around there was no opportunity for infidelity. Had there been such an opportunity, and Eve had divorced Adam, we wonder whether God would have still said, "It is not good that the man should be alone" (Gen. 2: 18). Would God have found a substitute or created another "helpmeet" for Adam? It is interesting to speculate.

Of course, the entire question is a bit ridiculous, because that is not the way things were. But the point is that divorce was never a part of the divine purpose. Divorce—the break-down of oneness—came after the fall, as did every other departure from the original design of the Creator.

The unity and goodness of God's plan for human beings was broken by the sin of Adam and Eve. This included God's plan for the companionship of one husband and one wife. Concubinage and polygamy seem to have been man's earliest devised way to undermine the Creator's plan. Abraham took a concubine (Gen. 16). Esau had many wives, and Jacob took two—as well as a couple of concubines. From there the practice seems to run wild, although it is clear that neither polygamy nor concubinage was endorsed by God.

By the time of Moses the problem of marital fragmentation had become so widespread that the lawgiver faced the necessity of some kind of legislation. Therefore, in order to maintain a semblance of order in the forming of a new nation, Moses arranged for a method of legalized divorce:

> When a man hath taken a wife, and married her, and it come to pass that she find no favor in his eyes, because he hath found some uncleanness in her: then let him write her a bill of divorcement, and give it in her hand, and send her out of his house. And when she is departed out of his house, she may go and be another man's wife (Deut. 24: 1-2).

As Jesus later explained to the Pharisees, this arrangement had nothing to do with divine reconsideration; it was entirely due to the "hardness of [their] hearts" (Matt. 19: 8). This does not mean he was ruling out the necessity of such a provision. Jesus was suggesting that people must never allow themselves to believe that their attempts at dissolving the marriage contract are divinely ordained. From the beginning God ordained marriage as a permanent relationship, and there is no way to alter that divine ideal. However, while marriages are made in heaven by God, they are lived out on earth by man. And man has never yet been able to achieve the standard of the Holy.

One of the great theologians of our time has observed, "Legal divorce is no part of the divine command concerning marriage, for this proclaims and requires its indissolubility. It belongs only to the institution of marriage. The human institution takes into account the possibility of marriages which have no divine foundation and constitution, which are not contracted and lived out in obedience to God's command, and which can therefore be dissolved. The whole weakness of marriage as an institution is revealed at this point."[3]

It is significant to note that, according to the Old Testament provision, only the husband could initiate divorce. Women had no rights; therefore, no wife was allowed to divorce her husband. When Jesus, in Matthew 19, spoke of a woman's divorcing her husband, he was referring to Greek and Roman customs—not Hebrew.

As the rabbinical schools of thought developed it was not surprising that disagreement regarding the correct interpretation of Deuteronomy 24: 1-2 should arise. The school of Shammai accepted fornication as the only valid reason for terminating marriage. Hillel, grandson of Shammai, was so liberal as to recognize almost anything which displeased the husband. His followers claimed that to burn the gravy, to fail to say the right thing, or to fail to look lovely were reasons enough for a woman to be divorced. Naturally, Hillel became the most popular interpreter for Hebrews who tended toward laxity!

When the religious leaders of Israel came to Jesus asking, "Is it lawful for a man to put away his wife for every cause?" (Matt. 19: 3), their question was an attempt to *test* him. What they were asking our Lord to do was to side with Hillel ("for every cause") or with Shammai. They wanted him to take sides in the theological debate. And according to this account in Matthew, Jesus cast his vote with Shammai in recognizing "fornication" (v. 9) as the only legitimate termination of a marriage. Guy Duty insists that the whole Bible is written in legalistic language and that Jesus was here endorsing the final law relating to marriage.[4]

But whether Jesus actually favored the position of Shammai over Hillel is doubtful. Our Lord was consistently concerned with cutting away the accumulations of the centuries and getting back to the original intent of the Father in heaven.

How often Jesus was forced to point out that regulations handed down from one generation to another were actually against the real law of God! Oral traditions which had been finally written down by the Hebrew scribes often enjoyed the same authority as the Word of God. Jesus was reproving the scribes and Pharisees for allowing this to happen when he said to them, "Why do ye also transgress the commandment of God by your tradition?" (Matt. 15: 3, Mark 7: 9).

Some students of the Bible believe that a scribe (or even Matthew himself) may have felt Jesus' condemnation of divorce without exception to be too severe. Thus, he took it upon himself to add the phrase, "except for fornication." We know that this kind of thing happened. Sometimes it was intended only as a scribal commentary on the text, but in time became a part of the text itself.

While it is impossible to know for sure whether the words, "except for fornication," were a scribal addition, it is interesting to note that Matthew's gospel is the only one which includes this phrase. The Lord's teaching on divorce and remarriage is recorded in Matthew 5: 31–32, Mark 10: 2–12, and Luke 16: 18. Neither Mark nor Luke, in recording the same comment of Jesus, includes the "except" clause.

If one is looking for a legalistic approach to divorce, he will choose Matthew's rendering of Jesus' statement. Carl F. H. Henry writes, "Jesus clearly counters reading easy and quick divorce into Mosaic legislation by categorically stating that unchastity is the only possible grounds for divorce."[5]

For one interested in what grace has to say, Mark and Luke will be favored. "Christ meant to inculcate a higher view of the sacredness of marriage than had been held by the rabbis of either school," observes W. R. Inge. "I do not think that He meant to lay down hard and fast rules. If a very hard case had been brought before Him, He might possibly have said, as He said about another commandment, 'Marriage was made for man, not man for marriage.'"[6]

On the surface it would seem that Mark and Luke are more rigid than Matthew, but we shall later see this a bit differently. Obviously, both approaches cannot be correct. Either Mark and Luke failed to include all that Jesus said in his

17

statement on divorce, or Matthew has suffered the addition of a well-meaning Christian scribe.

It has been suggested that the exception offered in the gospel of Matthew has nothing to do with marriage as we conceive of it today. Rather, the reference is said to be to betrothal or the engagement of a Jewish man and woman. The engagement was almost as binding as marriage. However, in the event of unchastity during this period, the one sinned against was free to break the relationship. This is why Joseph felt free to depart from Mary when he felt she had been unfaithful to him (Matt. 1: 18–19). According to this view, once the betrothed were married there was *no* provision left for divorce. In any event, it seems to be a fact needing no proof that Jesus gives no excuse for divorce.

Nothing at all is said about the "fornication" clause in Paul's lengthy discussion of Christian marriage in 1 Corinthians 7 or in his briefer references in Romans 7: 1–3. The only places in the New Testament where the exception is mentioned are Matthew 5: 32 and 19: 9. And here it is important to note that, in the fuller teaching in Matthew, Jesus confirms the original intent of God as recorded in Genesis 2: 24: "For this cause shall a man leave father and mother, and shall cleave to his wife, and they twain shall be one flesh" (19: 5). Then he adds, "What therefore God hath joined together, let not man put asunder" (19: 6). In light of this confirmation, it would be strange indeed if in the same teaching Jesus should contradict himself by making an exception (19: 9).

Another point which needs to be noted is that in this same passage our Lord answered the Pharisee's question as to why Moses arranged for a "bill of divorce" with a clear-cut and unambiguous statement. It was not at all what the Pharisees had hoped for: "Moses because of the hardness of your hearts suffered [permitted] you to put away your wives: but from the beginning it was not so" (19: 8). The natural continuation in the next verse would be as follows *without* the words here placed in brackets and italicized: "And I say unto you, Whosoever shall put away his wife, [*except it be for fornication*] and shall marry another, committeth adultery: and whoso marrieth her which is put away doth commit adultery" (19: 9).

It is not reasonable that Jesus would have admitted any exception to God's original plan. He had just insisted that, no matter what Moses did as a concession to a fallen race, divorce was not part of God's original plan. Albert Knudson suggests, "It is probable that the words, 'except for fornication,' in Matthew 5: 32 and 19: 9 were added to the text . . . and that Jesus himself allowed for no exception to his commandment of divorce. But if that be true, it would mean that he was speaking not as a lawgiver, but rather as an upholder of the moral ideal." [7]

For the benefit of persons unfamiliar with the matter of "scribal additions," it may be helpful to point out in the conclusion to this chapter that such was a quite common practice in early New Testament times. It was never a deliberate attempt to confuse or lead the reader astray. On the contrary, it was an honest effort to add a commentary on a statement which the scribe felt was unclear or easily misunderstood.

Another example of such "scribal additions" in the Sermon on the Mount is found in Matthew 5: 44, where the words, "do good to them that hate you," are omitted in many of the most ancient manuscripts. These words were inserted in the fourth or fifth century to bring the verse into verbal agreement with Luke 6: 28. In Matthew 6: 4, the word *openly* is a classic example of a scribe's attempt to improve on the teaching of our Lord. The addition of this adverb weakens the force of the truth Jesus is teaching. The conclusion to the model prayer in Matthew 6: 13, "For thine is the kingdom, and the power, and the glory, for ever," is not found in the best manuscripts. It was added so as to round out the prayer after the pattern of most Jewish liturgical prayers. Ultimately the addition was interpolated by transcribers to harmonize the text with the liturgies. What can be observed in these examples taken from the Sermon on the Mount is also to be seen throughout the New Testament.

Perhaps this is as good a place as any in a discussion of the biblical position on divorce to say a word about Paul's letter to Timothy (1 Tim. 3: 2), in which he states that a "bishop" is to be "the husband of one wife." This has been a hotly debated passage since earliest times. While there is no way to settle the dispute with any finality, it is likely that Paul is not so much dealing here with divorce as he is repudiating polygamy. Many Christians came out of pagan cultures in which a man had several wives or lived with mistresses and concubines. Thus the apostle is here insisting that any person assuming the role of spiritual leadership within the church must come to terms with the Judeo-Christian ideal of monogamous marriage (*one* man and *one* woman living together.)

Norman Geisler shows that he believes this to be the natural meaning of this passage when he prefaces a quotation of 1 Timothy 3: 2 with the following words: "The New Testament sets down monogamy as a precondition for church leaders." [8] It may also be said that this passage *endorses* marriage for him who would serve as pastor or "bishop," since the biblical arrangement helps offset the tendency toward moral laxity in the vulnerable role of spiritual adviser and counselor.

All of this is to say that 1 Timothy 3: 2 is probably a reference to polygamy (see Deut. 17: 17, Mal. 2: 15, Tit. 1: 6) and a rejection of such a lifestyle for the Christian overseer. If this is so, these words have little to do with setting a standard for clergymen which puts them in a class by themselves regarding divorce.

The Heart
of
Jesus' Teaching

So far in our study of the gospel narratives as they bear on the problem of divorce and/or remarriage, we have said nothing about the passage in the Sermon on the Mount recorded in Matthew 5, beginning with verse 27. The entire passage, including the latter portion which we have already looked at, is here quoted:

> Ye have heard that it was said by them of old time, Thou shalt not commit adultery: But I say unto you that whosoever looketh on a woman to lust after her hath committed adultery with her already in his heart. And if thy right eye offend thee, pluck it out, and cast it from thee: for it is profitable for thee that one of thy members should perish, and not that thy whole body would be cast into hell. And if thy right hand offend thee, cut it off, and cast it from thee: for it is profitable for thee that one of thy members should perish, and not that thy whole body would be cast into hell. It hath been said, Whosoever shall put away his wife, let him give her a writing of divorcement: But I say unto you, That whosoever shall put away his wife, saving for the cause of fornication, causeth her to commit adultery: and whosoever shall marry her that is divorced committeth adultery (Matt. 5: 27–32).

One of the most grievous abuses of Scripture is the tendency to interpret passages out of context. These verses must be related to the total discourse dealing with the law (Matt. 5: 17–48). Furthermore, they must be read with the intention of understanding the real truth Christ was teaching.

Practically every treatment of the Sermon on the Mount

assumes that Jesus was laying a new moral requirement upon his followers, a new law to supercede that of the Old Covenant. Needless to say, the Sermon on the Mount does set up an ethical standard of righteousness—the highest possible—which clarifies exactly what God's design for the Christian community is to be. But we are amiss if we think that God's acceptance of us hinges on how well we perform.

What our Lord is doing in Matthew 5 is amplifying the laws of Moses for the purpose of declaring their divine meaning. In each instance, he shows that there is more to keeping the law than the religious leaders thought. While the common people of the land knew they failed to keep the law, the religious leaders insisted that they themselves were successful. But Jesus settled the matter once and for all in the Sermon. *No one,* in view of what Jesus says about the laws of Moses, can ever again claim to have kept them. "In face of a standard which requires more of us than we are capable of performing, and only then," says Paul Ramsey, "is the righteousness of those great and noble men, the scribes and pharisees, exceeded." [9]

In these verses we have a fresh look at several of the laws. It will be noted that all the laws mentioned have a direct bearing on man in his relationships with other men. We learn, for example, that the commandment, "Thou shalt not kill," is not obeyed by avoiding the overt act of murder. To be angry with another person is all it takes to be guilty (vv. 21–22). This is because the desire of one's heart is what God looks at—and murder stems from anger, hostility, and hatred. The "anger" referred to here is related to any kind of hateful feelings, resentment, or desire for retaliation.

What was said in the last chapter about the "except" clause in the divorce passage must be said in reference to this excerpt about anger. The words "without a cause" weaken the very truth which Jesus is seeking to impart. Here again a scribe has probably been at work to lessen the severity of Jesus' words. These three words are not found in many of the best and oldest manuscripts! Obviously, if our Lord is saying that man is guilty of murder by being angry, he is not going to make an exception which opens the door to all shades of interpretation. He is not going to suggest that there may be *a cause* for breaking the law! Christ's amplification of this commandment means that we are all guilty.

What the Lord does with the law against murder, he does also with the laws against adultery (vv. 27–32), perjury (vv. 33–37), retaliation (vv. 38–42), and hatred toward enemies (vv. 43–47). The last verse (v. 48) of chapter 5 clinches the impossibility of achieving the righteous standard of God (the standard so succinctly presented in the Ten Commandments): "Be ye, therefore, perfect, even as your Father, who is in heaven, is perfect."

Our Lord is simply saying that if man expects to be declared righteous on the basis of his keeping of the law, he must understand first of all how high the law is. And when he recognizes *that*, there will be no further pride left in him. Who among us would dare presume that we are "perfect even as [our] Father"? Paul says in Romans 4:2 that if man is saved by his works (which obviously he is not) he may have something to brag about, "but not before God." We are all in the process of developing toward maturity, but that is a divine gift which will not be realized in its Godlike completeness until the resurrection.

The law was never given by God with the expectation that man would perfectly obey it. Paul says the law is a "schoolmaster to bring us unto Christ" (Gal. 3:24). That is, when the law does what it was destined to do, it will convince man of his guilt and helplessness to remove it. Then, hopefully, he will turn to God's remedy which has nothing to do with man's achievement. The law is powerless to do anything about our sin. It can only reveal it in all its utter ugliness. One verse in Romans makes this very clear: "By the deeds of the law there shall no flesh be justified in his sight: for by the law is the knowledge of sin" (Rom. 3:20).

The Sermon on the Mount is not a map to heaven. We do not get right with God by living up to these high standards. Multitudes of people profess to live by the Ten Commandments, never realizing that the Sermon on the Mount makes such success impossible. On the other hand, many persons are defeated in their Christian discipleship because they have read the Sermon and given up! And there are still others who rationalize away the severity of Matthew 5 so as to make themselves appear to measure up. All this is so self-defeating. That is what always happens when fallen man attempts to prove his power to live as if unfallen.

In clarifying and amplifying the law in the Sermon, Jesus is saying to us that we must run to the cross, because only God can do what must be done. Only he can impute righteousness to us. And that happens when we stop trying to be good enough for God, when we acknowledge our sin. Christ is the only perfect Son of God, the only righteous One as judged by the law. He kept the law and thus fulfilled it. Now it can no longer condemn us if we trust him to clear our account. Who else could do it except him who has paid the debt?

The Sermon on the Mount, then, like the Ten Commandments, was given to drive us to the cross for forgiveness. Christ, not an ethical code of behavior, is our salvation.

This brings us to the teachings of Jesus on divorce, as related to the whole of his discourse on grace and law in chapter 5. All men and women are guilty of breaking the law at some point. And James insists, "Whosoever shall keep the whole law, and yet offend in one point, he is guilty of all" (James 2: 10). Some harbor anger in their hearts, some are lustful, some untruthful, some unloving. But not one of us is perfect. Is there anyone who is characterized by absolute love, or truth, or purity? Of course not!

There is no justifiable reason for isolating divorce and/or remarriage from the rest of the condemnations in this chapter, as if one somehow is worse than the others. While some find their greatest weakness at the point of anger, some find it at the point of carelessness with truth, and others at the point of marital failure. God demands that we be perfect if acceptable on our merits. Who is? And what right do we have to label divorce as being more permanently contaminating than other sin?

Perhaps the reason we tend toward thinking of divorce and/or remarriage as worse is that we often view it as a *con-*

tinuing evil. Even if a divorced person remains single, he is assumed to be living in a state of *static* sin, the act itself having condemned the rest of life. If such a one remarries, he is said to be living in a state of *dynamic* sin, because the new marriage is a continuous act of adultery. Either way, he is an unfortunate creature, having destined himself to life on a dead-end street. For all practical purposes, he is declared hopeless by legalism.

The irony, however, is that we should isolate one particular sin from the list and treat it more severely than the rest. The whole point of chapter 5 in Matthew is that man cannot attain this righteous standard. Only Christ can do this. He is the perfect One. In union with him by faith we are accepted by God (justified) in spite of our failures and shortcomings as fallen creatures. We are all thrown on the mercy of God— the divorced and/or remarried included—if we are to survive the fires of judgment upon sin.

Divorce and/or remarriage is sin. It has been since the beginning of the human creation. To break the "oneness" of man and woman joined in wedlock is to reverse the Creator's original design. That is rebelliousness, which is the root of all sin. Nothing we can say will change these facts. But what has been said of divorce must be said also of every departure from God's will.

The glory of the Gospel is that God forgives sin and gives us a new start. Divorce and/or remarriage is not the unpardonable sin. It must be remembered that God does not forgive us and then hold our failures over our heads. People may do that—even church people—but not God. To the church people of his day, who had brought a poor woman caught in the act of adultery, Jesus said, "He that is without sin among you, let him first cast a stone at her" (John 8: 7). And, also in the Gospel of John, we hear our Lord saying, "God sent not his Son into the world to condemn the world; but that the world through him might be saved" (John 3: 17).

This has always been the way of God. Since the beginning, he has been a God of compassion who desires to forgive people and let them begin again. The adultery and murder of Uriah by King David was as bad as—if not worse than (in man's value system)—divorce. Yet God honored the marriage of David and Bathsheba after the repentance of the sinners (2 Sam. 11–12).

God did not reckon David's sin with Bathsheba as damning guilt, but freely forgave him. He so fully forgave that he gave Bathsheba another son (Solomon) and bestowed a love upon him which gave him the name Jedidiah, which means beloved of the Lord (2 Sam. 12: 24, 25). Furthermore, God put Bathsheba in the genealogy of Christ (Matt. 1: 6) and called David a man "after his own heart" (1 Sam. 13: 14). This is what grace does. Only the condemning, self-righteous, grace-ignoring would beg to disagree with the compassion of the Lord.

It is important to note that if God were this forgiving during the covenant of law we may rightly assume that he would still be as compassionate in a day of grace!

How Jesus Treated the Divorced

It must be observed from the outset that no case of divorce *per se* (unless it be the woman of Sychar) is to be found among the Lord's confrontations as recorded in the New Testament. It would help if such a case had been preserved on the sacred page. But the fact that there is no such passage means that "there is no way to know for sure how Jesus or Paul would have answered some of the contemporary questions concerning divorce."[10] We must deduce the specific from the general.

In the Sermon on the Mount, Christ speaks of divorce and remarriage as adultery. Since we have no specific instance of how he handled divorce, we must study the cases of adultery which are recorded. A look at the way our Lord treated people who had been worsted by sexual laxity is quite illuminating.

It is interesting that, although Jesus referred to adultery numerous times in his teaching (Matt. 5: 28–32; Mark 10: 11, 19; Luke 16: 18; Luke 18: 11; etc.), only two cases of his dealing with personal adultery are preserved for us. They are both found in John's Gospel.

John 4: 5–30 records Jesus' conversation with a woman of Samaria who had been married five times (presumably divorced from all five) and was living with a sixth man out of wedlock. Nowhere did Jesus treat her as if she had committed a sin which needed to ruin the rest of her life. Nowhere did he tell her to go back to her husband (which one would it be?) This does not mean he condoned a lifestyle such as she had been practicing. But he did recognize there was no way

27

to undo what had been done. And Jesus was always more interested in what a person could become than in what he had been.

Whether the Samaritan woman became a follower of Jesus we do not know. It appears from the account that she probably did, but nowhere are we emphatically told as much. Neither do we know what she did about her marital disarray. If she became a Christian, we may assume that she married the man she had been living with (or broke off the relationship entirely), and began a new life. But again, we are not told.

The other incident involving adultery is in John 8: 1–11, a passage which some students of the Bible do not believe to be part of the original text. Be that as it may, the story is in keeping with the spirit of Jesus as we see him elsewhere upon the New Testament page.

A woman caught in the act of adultery was brought to Jesus by the scribes and Pharisees with the reminder that Moses' law demanded her stoning (Lev. 20: 10; Deut. 22: 22–24; Num. 5: 11–31). John tells us they were testing Jesus (v. 6) to see whether he would ignore the law. What happened, however, is that Jesus ignored the religious leaders themselves. Writing in the sand with his finger, the Lord invited the man without sin to be the first to cast a stone. What he wrote we do not know, but it may have been the particular sins of the accusers. Whatever it was, not a man dared throw his stones.

Turning to the frightened adulterous woman, Jesus asked whether anyone had condemned her. Seeing her accusers gone, the trembling woman acknowledged the obvious fact that no one was left to pronounce the judgment of God except the Lord himself. Then Jesus said, "Neither do I condemn thee: go, and sin no more" (v. 11).

In each of these instances, Jesus conveyed a similar attitude. The Master was not concerned about the past—only about the life which remained. His injunction to "sin no more" means that the old lifestyle of habitual looseness was to be terminated. The sinner could begin anew.

Often the church finds it difficult to let such persons "begin again." Their past is continually held against them. And this is especially true if the person happens to have been divorced. At times it almost appears that the church can forgive and forget any sexual laxity before marriage, but a divorced person will never be permitted to live a normal life again. Yet it is the union which is consummated in a sexual relationship, not some legal contract or ceremony, which makes a man and a woman "one flesh" (1 Cor. 6: 16). Therefore, divorce is no worse than any other sexual dishonesty which breaks apart the divine union.

Our Lord was compassionate with persons caught in this particular kind of sin because he knew the terrible stigma which the religious placed upon them. One sin is no worse than another in God's sight. Only man sets up a scale for determining the seriousness of varying sins. It is the wrongness of fallen man's heart that God sees, not the multitude of sins that are symptomatic of his fallenness.

If the Father in heaven forgives at all, would he attach strings to such forgiveness? What kind of forgiveness would that be? When he forgives the past, it is as if it had never been. The divorced person, when forgiven, is treated as if he had never been married. Therefore, all legalism in dealing with divorced people is foreign to the spirit of Jesus.

Note what a mess any remedy other than forgiveness would cause! Some people are so legalistic as to argue that the only way divorce can be corrected is by remarriage to the original partner. Granted, that would be the best solution—if it could be arranged. However, it is not usually a practical suggestion, because one or both of the partners is often unwilling for any such reconciliation to take place.

Some argue that anyone who has been divorced and remarried must right his wrong by leaving the second person to whom he is bound by legal wedlock and being reunited with the first. What a complicated arrangement that can be! Two wrongs do not make a right. Furthermore, suppose there are children by the new marriage! And what if the first wife or husband is married again? While this may be a solution from a purely legal viewpoint it has no room in it for human compassion, nor does it have any understanding of the complexity of such a dilemma. As long as we insist on the letter of the marriage law, there is no way to approach the ever-present reality of divorce in our society.

It is the responsibility of the church to condemn sin without fear. The world must know what God's will is, and what happens when we disregard that will. But the church must not be so idealistic as to be out of touch with reality. As long as man lives in a fallen world he will "come short of the glory of God" (Rom. 3: 23). Therefore, it is necessary that the church meet man where he is with the forgiveness of God. God hates divorce (Mal. 2: 16) but he loves the divorced person!

This does not mean that anything goes. It only means that there are some predicaments into which sin gets men and women out of which there is no way to escape except through forgiveness. God must wipe the slate clean, because man cannot erase his guilt. And if God does clean the slate, the church can do no less than accept it.

The laws of God are perfect, but the people who live under them are not. And perfect laws will never be kept by imperfect men and women. By now it should be clear to all but the most blatantly self-righteous that the laws of God are higher than any man's achievement. But Christians are not in bondage to divine law. God has seen to that himself. Since Christ has come, our God does not condemn us with legal prohibitions. He is not an attorney bent on proving us guilty. He is a Father who treats us with compassion and love. It is a good thing for us that God is more merciful with his children than his children are with each other.

II.
What Are the Problems of the Divorced?

What Would You Do?

Before we can minister to divorced people, we must come to an understanding of their special problems. The case histories that follow and the "Check-on-Yourself" section at the end of the chapter are designed to provide insight into the plight of the divorced and to stimulate thinking on how the church can help meet their needs.

Case One:

Sue had her first date with Marvin while a sophomore in high school. It was love at first sight. Although she had been to the movies and school dances with other boys, Sue had never felt about anyone the way she felt about Marvin. Once she and Marvin began seeing each other, there was just no time for anyone else. The romance developed so rapidly that within six months both were talking about marriage. Since the parents on both sides were opposed to marriage before graduation, Sue and Marvin decided to run off and "tie the knot." At this time, Marvin was seventeen and Sue sixteen.

For a few months everything was beautiful. The parents accepted the arrangement and tried to help with the finances while their married children continued their schooling. Soon, however, Marvin was forced to drop out of high school and take full-time employment. It was not long until that became old. While other boys were playing basketball, he was having to work to support a wife. And Sue? She was six months pregnant and dreaming of the fun she used to have at girl parties with her school friends. That was all over. The responsibilities were more than either of them could handle. They were just not ready for that kind of settling down.

It soon became clear that neither of these two people were even remotely prepared for marriage. And what they had thought was love was an infatuation that would have passed if they had given their relationship time to cool.

Sue is now twenty-two, divorced, and the mother of a four-year-old son. Marvin is remarried and living in a distant city. There are many lonely nights for Sue. In spite of her love for little Marvin, there is no companionship or sharing of her adult life. And little Marvin is growing up without a father. Sometimes Sue feels alone, insecure, and frustrated with the emptiness of her days.

Having been taught that divorced persons cannot marry again without incurring the wrath of God, Sue is afraid even to accept a dinner invitation with a single male. There is no future except the bleak prospects of years of suffering in loneliness for a mistake in judgment she made while still too young to understand the responsibilities of marriage.

Case Two:

After twenty-seven years of marriage Bob and Helen finally separated. Two years later their divorce was finalized. There had been no hint of unfaithfulness on the part of either person; had that been the case the problem might have been easier to handle.

Bob was a hard worker. He made a good living, and the family always had anything they wanted. Bob did not drink or waste his earnings. In fact, he was an exemplary man with few bad habits. But he worked the night shift and was seldom with his wife and children. During the day, the children had to be quiet so Dad could sleep. They could not have friends over after school. And Helen? She spent the nights alone and the days with Bob asleep. The children thought of their father as a "stranger who paid the bills."

Helen had tried many times to get Bob to change jobs. There had been several opportunities for day work, but the night pay was better and Bob would not hear of earning less money. Although his wife explained that some things are worth more than money—things like sitting before the fire together, going to dinner and a movie in the evening, playing ball with the boys—there was no changing Bob's mind.

Finally, Helen could take no more of being married to a man with whom she seldom had the chance to share her life. She left him, thinking perhaps he would come to his senses. Eighteen months later, however, he was still wrapped up in his night job. Even when threatened with divorce, there was no change.

Now Helen is forty-nine years old, and the children are grown and married. She sees her children enjoying happiness which she never had. They would like to see their mother find happiness with someone new. But Helen is afraid to risk it. What if the second marriage did not work, either? Should she have stayed with Bob and suffered through another fifteen or twenty years until he decided to retire? And what would happen to Bob? The guilt will not go away.

Case Three:

Roger and Alice were married nearly seventeen years. They were both active in their church, where Alice still teaches a class of young girls. Having grown up in a very strict home where sex was never mentioned, Alice always had the feeling that sex was not to be enjoyed. There seemed to be somthing dirty about the whole thing. Her home church had been rigid in its approach to boy-girl relationships. There had been a dress code which was supposed to protect young couples from temptation. Holding hands had been strictly forbidden, since it might lead to something "worse."

Roger's background had been quite different. It is no wonder that Roger could not understand the coldness of his wife. Every night, she either had a headache or was so tired she managed to fall asleep as soon as her head touched the pillow. If he tried to woo his wife, Roger was accused of being oversexed.

Being a normal male with typical human drives, Roger had found life with Alice less and less satisfying. One night he jokingly warned her that she was going to drive him to find love in a brothel. She replied in such a way as to cause him to believe that she would not object if he would only leave her alone.

The years only made matters worse. Roger did not want to be unfaithful, but what was he to do? It was soon apparent that Alice had not meant what she said. When she discovered her husband's unfaithfulness, she took their twelve-year-old daughter and went to live with her parents. She would not divorce Roger, because divorce was against her religious convictions.

For three years now, Roger has lived apart from his wife. He is not free to marry again. There have been several illicit affairs with young women, but that is not the kind of life he wants. What he really wants is a *wife* who will love him and make a home where he can be a husband. Sometimes Roger does not know what to do next. His life is mixed up; there are times when he does not know whether he even believes in God anymore. And of course he stopped going to church long ago.

Case Four:

Everybody said theirs was the perfect marriage. They seemed to be so perfectly matched. But things are not always what they seem. Inside the Smith household things were not going well. Frank and Shirley were short with each other. It was obvious that Shirley was restless. Often Frank would come home from work and she would not be there. There would be no dinner and Shirley would have a new excuse.

One morning a few weeks before their eleventh anniversary, Shirley nervously blurted out at the breakfast table, "I want a divorce!" Once she had said that, there was little difficulty in telling her whole story. Shirley had been having an affair with a local businessman for eight months. She admitted that there was no longer any love for Frank. She loved the other man and would not be content until she had a divorce and was able to marry him.

Although he had known something was wrong, Frank was shocked and hurt to hear his wife's admission of unfaithfulness. The whole thing was a severe blow to his manhood. He did not want a divorce, and refused to give in for several months. Nothing seemed to help. His offer to forgive her and let bygones be bygones only humiliated Shirley and drove her farther from him. At last, his back against the wall, Frank agreed to the divorce.

Shirley is now living with the businessman, whom she has not married. After five years, Frank is still living alone in a rented room. There were no children. Frank's friends try to get him involved with people and invite him to social functions, but he stays in his room most of the time when he is not working. It is obvious that Shirley will never be back. Some are afraid that Frank is developing suicidal tendencies. Something needs to be done before it is too late.

Case Five:

Bruce was a bachelor. At thirty-eight years of age, he had amassed a small fortune. He drove a flashy sports car and lived in a plush apartment overlooking the lake. He had worked hard since getting his first job with an accounting firm, with which he still worked after nearly twenty years. Although he dated occasionally, there had never been anyone with whom there was more than a passing friendship. Bruce was the talk of the community. He would be a great "catch" for someone. Anyone who had worked himself up from assistant janitor to one of the leading accountants in his city was bound to make a responsible husband.

One day a new woman was hired for a position as secretary at the accounting office where Bruce worked. She was not a beauty queen, but there was something regal, something very appealing about this thirty-three-year-old widow. Her husband had died of cancer two years earlier. Little by little, Bruce was drawn to her. They had not had more than a half-dozen dates when Jane was swept off her feet by his proposal of marriage.

The neighborhood could not believe it, but everyone was happy. The wedding was lavish. Jane moved into the plush "bachelor's pad," and life was again beautiful for her after so many lonely nights. It was not easy learning to cope with a bachelor's ways. But the greater difficulty was Bruce's. He just couldn't adjust to being married. Life had been so different as a bachelor. He had come and gone as he pleased for so long that being responsible for and to a wife was more than he could handle.

After the first month things began to sour. By the end of six months of hectic maladjustment, the glamor was all gone; they could not stand the sight of each other. Most of their time was spent arguing. There was nothing left to do but separate. After eighteen months, Jane had her divorce, and Bruce was a happy bachelor again. But Jane? There were more lonely nights and empty dreams. Maybe someday someone else would come along. If so, how could she be sure? And what about her living husband? Would a third marriage be a sin?

Check on Yourself:

1) What were your feelings as you read these cases? Write them down.

2) If these people came to you for advice, what would you say?

3) What do you think would be the position of your pastor in each of these cases?

4) If the pastor should perform a marriage for any one of these persons, how would your church respond?

5) After studying the biblical teaching on divorce and viewing each of the case studies in the light of it, how do you imagine Jesus would handle them?

6) Would you handle any of these cases differently if the victim were your son or daughter? The child of a dear friend? A Roman Catholic? A Protestant? A Jew? A Negro?

7) How do you think your feelings might be changed if you yourself were the unfortunate victim in any one of these cases?

8) What could a church action group do to help persons like these find new life and wholeness?

Divorce
and
Loneliness

Among the many haunting problems of the divorced man or woman is loneliness. Loneliness arises from the frustration of having to live in a condition not meant by the heavenly Father. When a marriage breaks apart, a man or woman may feel as if half of his or her life is gone. If two people become one in marriage, then either spouse becomes only one-half in divorce. The basic unit of existence is one—not two and certainly not a half!

In no way is this meant to be an offense to the person who is divorced. Many such persons learn to make a good life out of the pieces of their broken marriages, whether they try matrimony again or not. And we must take our hats off to them when they succeed, because it is far from easy. Our point is only that the divorced person is at least subconsciously aware that a basic and fundamental part of his life is gone. He no longer feels quite complete after divorce. Ironically enough, he may feel happier—if the marriage was a miserable arrangement—but he still senses a decrease in wholeness.

It is true that divorced persons do not always appear lonely, but appearances may be deceiving. Under the broadest smile and behind the heartiest laugh may beat an aching heart. There is nothing unusual about forcing the appearance of happiness. Millions of sad, lonely folk do it every day.

Even in a crowd, a person can feel "out of it." At a party, the divorced man or woman may feel like an island in the sea. Obviously, the divorced person gets the impression that he is out of place with most of his married friends. And nobody wants to be a "spare tire." For that reason, divorced people often find it easier to decline invitations to social functions than to accept them. Only at a party arranged solely for single or divorced people does the once-married person find himself comfortable. And that is an artificial substitute for real social living.

Of course, some married people are lonely, too; they may have made an unfortunate selection of mates or experienced some loss which cannot be replaced. But the loneliness of the divorced person is especially acute. He may not be able to live with his chosen mate—there may even be a real dislike—but he is nevertheless lonely when he loses what has been a natural part of his life.

There is a striking similarity between the emotional response to divorce and the response to the death of a loved one. If one can be considered worse than the other, it is safe to say that the trauma of divorce is worse than the trauma of death, because rejection is involved. I have experienced the untimely death of a much-beloved wife, and I know what a crushing experience bereavement can be. But in death the will of the deceased is not a factor in the awful separation. In divorce that will is the one crucial thing—there is the haunting knowledge that someone actually *wants* to end a marriage, that someone is rejecting another. Regardless how stoic a man or a woman may be, this is the kind of thing that jabs like a knife in the quiet moments and lonely hours.

Sometimes the grief response may not set in immediately. The newly divorced are apt to be so relieved to get out of an unhappy situation that they feel fifty pounds lighter. Only later does the weight of what has happened sink in. And when that moment comes, it is like waking up to reality and crying, "How did this happen to me? And why?" At this point the divorced person feels alone, despondent, and hopeless.

Even the person who has initiated a marital break-up in order to regain his freedom may be far from pleased with his new role. Freedom can be terribly lonely—actually terrifying. Only when we are responsible *to* someone else as well as *for* him do we discover the meaning of life in relationship.

To know that there is no one to come home to in the evening

41

or no one to prepare dinner for—that is hard to handle. One who has been married finds himself planning to share some news with his spouse, only to be stabbed awake by the fact that no one will be there. This is true for the divorced as well as for the bereaved.

At night especially does such a person suffer. He dreams of happier times, only to awaken clutching the pillow in his arms. The tears may run at night from eyes which were forced to twinkle during the day. And the wells which appeared dry during waking hours may suddenly overflow in the darkness and loneliness of the early morning hours.

Loneliness is a way of life for persons whose marriages have come tumbling down. Even when there are children in the house—and they *do* help—there is still that empty place no one else can fill.

The person who would witness to these people about Christ's offer of salvation must be keenly aware of and sensitive to the loneliness of the divorced. Christ had a deep compassion for men and women suffering from this condition. He must have sensed the lonely plight of the woman of Samaria. She had come alone to draw water at noonday, when the sun was hottest. The other women all came in the evening, when the atmosphere had cooled. But not this woman. She came when no one else would be apt to be there, because she was even more lonely in a crowd of people who scorned her for what she had done than she was by herself in the middle of the day (John 4).

Jesus talked to the woman of Samaria when no one else would. That was because he cared. Likewise, he cared for the lonely woman caught in adultery (John 8), for the mother in Nain who had lost her son (Luke 7: 11–17), for Mary and Martha after the death of Lazarus (John 11), for his own mother and his disciple John when he was dying on the cross (John 19: 25–27).

While the Christian has a Savior to offer to the divorced, he has also to give himself in love and compassion. Never should he rush in where angels fear to tread. Rather, he would do well to cross on tiptoe the threshold of lonely, aching hearts.

This is not to say that the Christian should be of sad countenance. Far from it. Christians never lead anyone to Christ unless they look and act redeemed! But with special sensitivity the witness should present him who bore our griefs and shared our loneliness upon Calvary. He is the companion for every lonely soul, the One who knew better than any other what it is like to be forsaken, rejected, and ignored.

Divorce
and
Guilt

Loneliness is not the only frustration endured by the divorced—nor is it the worst. A king-sized burden of guilt often weighs such people down. Guilt comes from the consciousness of having done something wrong, something out of keeping with divine or social expectations. Even though a divorce may be the best of all possible solutions to a hopelessly shattered relationship, there is still a sense of guilt. Divorce was just never meant to be, and to experience such a thing is to be aware of standing against the will of God.

Guilt may show itself in many different forms. First, a person may feel that, if he had done things differently, the marriage might still be intact. He may blame himself for what has happened. And that is a hard thing to live with. To think that one might have avoided so tragic an end to what began as a happy adventure is a crushing blow. Whether a different approach earlier would have made a significant difference can never be determined with any certainty. And it is the uncertainty which makes the situation so difficult.

A divorced person may also carry a heavy load of guilt about what divorce has done to his children. If there are no children, divorce is usually much simpler. But it is often the case that innocent children become victims in a tragedy over which they have no control. It is not normal and healthy for a child to be in the custody of one parent and be visited by the other only on weekends or special occasions. Such a child experiences a fragmentation of his inner self which militates against his right to a wholesome home and family life. Divorced parents know this. And with that knowledge goes a certain amount of guilt.

Often there is also a degree of moral and spiritual guilt about divorce, depending on the depth of the divorced person's religious beliefs. That may range all the way from mild feelings of divine disapproval to more extreme cases in which a person fears the wrath of God for what he has done.

This sense of guilt in the sight of God may cause the divorced person to attend religious services more often, in an effort to compensate for what has happened. Or it may produce the opposite reaction; he may terminate all contacts with the church because of his humiliation and hopelessness. The Christian community cannot afford to ignore these people. Nor can we continue to scold them for what has been done. There is no future in that for the church or the divorced person.

The Protestant Reformation of the sixteenth century caught fire due to a rediscovery of the biblical truth that man is justified by faith *alone,* without the deeds of the law (Rom. 3: 28). What a release it was when the people learned that God would justify (treat as righteous) anyone who would trust Christ's death as total payment for man's sin! And what a greater joy it was to learn that all men are sinners—both before and after conversion—and that the difference lies not in becoming morally sinless but in trusting Jesus Christ to do for us what we cannot do for ourselves.

This means that every day the Christian is enabled to begin again. He fails at many points, but at no time has he committed an unpardonable sin, as long as he keeps his faith in the power of Christ to save. There is no need for any man to exist under the weight of guilt when Christ forgives and accepts. God accepts us, unrighteous as we are, in our union with his righteous Son—*as if* we were righteous.

What does all this say to the divorced person? Frankly, it says that divorce is a sin—but not beyond forgiveness. It is no different than any other sin in the sight of God. It is the fallenness of humanity which causes divorce; therefore, it is that fallen condition which is the source of the problem. When God forgives, he deals with the evil in our hearts which causes us to reveal symptoms such as divorce. Divorce is not dynamic—continuing to make us guilty. It is cancelled out completely by our faith in Christ's death.

When a divorced person remarries, he begins again—if he is in Christ—as if all the past were not really there. Although the act of divorce and/or remarriage is adultery, Christ forgives adultery as he forgives any other sin, and life begins all over again.

The church must help the divorced to get rid of their guilt. We must never try to increase it or make it permanent. That is not at all the business of the church. It is the Christian's business to lead people into the love and forgiveness of the Redeemer.

Like Christ, the Christian community must assist persons who have been worsted by living in a fallen world to find a new life. Never let it be said of us that we drive the wedge of guilt deeper into a person's mind. The admonition of Christ must be sounded again and again by the church—"Go and sin no more"—but we must never lead people to believe we mean they have to "undo" their divorce. In most cases that would be humanly impossible. Nor does this admonition mean that a divorced person can never again enter into wedlock, or that a second marriage must be anulled in order to restore the first.

When Jesus explained that divorce was instituted because of the "hardness of [our] hearts," he was not suggesting that such a provision for human "hardness" is no longer needful. As long as man lives in a fallen world, there will be divorce, and the necessity for some kind of legal and social recognition of it. Christ was only pointing out the original plan of God as being without provision for the disruption.

Divorce was never, and still is not, the will of God. But God deals with us on the basis of what and where we are as fallen creatures. After all, there would be nothing to forgive if people were not subject to this "hardness of heart."

Our message to the world must be that no one has to put up with unresolved guilt. God's grace is sufficient to meet and conquer every sin man is capable of committing. That includes divorce and remarriage.

Divorce
and
Insecurity

Insecurity is a frightening thing to face. To be insecure is to have nothing to tie to, to be adrift in a shoreless sea. If there were only something definite in the threatening days and years which stretch out before a person who is unaccustomed to going it alone! But usually there is nothing of the sort to hang on to. The divorced person often feels at the mercy of an impersonal world, helpless before the hopeless advance of time.

There are many kinds of insecurity. Financial insecurity often plagues the divorced—the difficulties of supporting children on reduced income, the loss of property in the divorce settlement. Shortage of money can shadow a divorced person's whole existence.

But emotional insecurity is an even greater problem for the divorced. Man and woman are made for each other, made to share all of life—the good and the bad. Every life has its share of unsteadying experiences, and it is much easier to face those moments when there is some support from a mate. There is security in the knowledge that someone else is in on what happens, that one is not roughing it by himself.

A mother with her children (although the mother does not always get court custody) may feel the pressure and fear of the future without a husband and father in calling distance. Even a father who has a job which takes care of his own needs as well as his family's may suffer the trauma of insecurity. He may never admit it, for fear of sounding unmanly, but it can be there, nevertheless.

It should be fairly obvious that, for a divorced person, the emotional security provided by parents, friends, or children cannot replace the special feeling of security which is reserved for the married state. While one may feel no need of this emotional undergirding as long as he or she remains single, once marriage has been consummated it is a different story. Divorce can never erase the need for the marriage relationship. All divorce ever does is make an unnatural break legal, in providing the *right* for a return to the single state. *Returning* to that state is something else entirely.

Aloneness, which was discussed in an earlier section, is its own insecurity. To be thrown suddenly into the world alone, after having lived in the company of a loving wife or husband, is frightening even for the strongest person. Actually, this is true whether the marriage was a good one or not. The man or woman who cannot wait for the day of legal freedom from a spouse is usually fooling himself. It is not so great as we think to be independent, especially when that freedom destroys a part of one's emotional security.

Although our concern here is primarily for the man or woman who is divorced, we must not overlook the emotional insecurity which is suffered by children in a broken home. Everything about life's balance is thrown off-center and jeopardized by a marital breakdown. Clearly, this ought to correct any idea that persons either directly or indirectly involved in a divorce can live as if nothing were changed.

If there is anything with which the church of Jesus Christ should be sympathetic, it is this ever-increasing universal problem of insecurity. The whole crisis of personal identity which has swept the world is closely related to this lack of personal security. Man finds his identity only when he experiences the security which comes in knowing that someone takes a special interest in his well-being. No one can know himself except in relationship with someone else. And security has a way of losing its meaning unless it can be shared.

If Jesus was right—and as Christians we accept that without reservation—we are to see God's will for his creation as having no place within it for insecurity. He wills us happiness and peace. It is not a part of his plan that anyone should experience the trauma which divorce brings with it. Since man does not always abide by the will of God in this fallen world, he brings upon himself suffering never intended by a loving Father. But this does not mean that our heavenly Father abandons us. Rather, he is so hurt with us in our sin that he has sent his Son to assure us of forgiveness and the good news of a second chance for happiness and security.

Is it not correct to say that the time has come for the church to reconsider its attitude and approach to the growing problem of divorce? Our world is bursting at the seams with suffering. What it needs today is not harshness and condemnation, but compassion and forgiveness.

There is no reason for followers of Jesus Christ to make people feel afraid and insecure. Yet that is what we do when the church continually leaves the impression that there is something about divorce which stigmatizes a person and makes it impossible for him ever to live a normal life again. It is our business to show love and forgiveness and to aid the divorced in rebuilding his life on a more secure foundation in Christ.

III.
How Can the Church Minister to the Divorced?

Structuring
the Church to
Deal with Divorce

For a long time, the Christian community has drawn its pious cloaks about itself and made it hard for the person of the world to find God. While God has been open and forgiving with the human race, often his church has stood in the way and blocked the world's access to the Father in heaven. This is like the head (Christ) willing one thing and the body (the church) doing another. Of course, we Christians have not meant to be that way. We want to rightly represent our Lord, but we are afraid of compromise, fearful that someone may think that we condone sin because we are compassionate. Nonetheless, if we would be like our Master we must take that risk.

Until the church stops acting as if divorce and/or remarriage were unpardonable sins, there will be no chance that this innumerable host of hurt people will consider us seriously. By our attitudes, we have caused these persons to become either bitter toward the church or to condemn themselves unmercifully within that fellowship. Certainly Jesus would not have his church turn people off. Neither would he expect us to censure such unfortunate people. If the church is Christ's body in the world, then it should be assumed that our approach to divorce would be like his. And Jesus' approach was compassion.

There is no reason why divorced Christians should be refused positions of leadership in the church. Perfect men and women have never been available for any task! Why should this particular imperfection be considered more serious than others? By what standard of values do we decide the degree of a specific symptom of our fallenness? All of this is to say that the church of our Lord Jesus Christ must exhibit the love and compassion which characterizes our Head. We must stop making a distinction between divorced persons and people who have managed to escape such a tragedy. After all, God is the Judge; we are not given any authority for usurping his right to evaluate his own (Rom. 14:4). Some of the most Christlike people I have known have been divorced and remarried. What a loss to the church if these people were consigned to some "lower level" because of sin which God has already forgiven.

If we are to witness to the divorced and minister to their needs, we are going to have to forget our concern for protecting the sanctity of our institution. We must remember that people are more important to our heavenly Father than any tradition—no matter how long cherished. It is a matter of grace that is adequate for every person, including the divorced!

There are many concrete ways the church can be structured to effectively minister to the divorced. Divorced persons often do not become a part of a Sunday School class or special interest group because they feel left out—like a fifth wheel or a spare tire. In most churches there are no classes for people whose marriages have been broken. This is a serious neglect. Such a class ought to be developed—one in which widows and widowers, divorced people, and unmarried persons would feel at home with one another. And the church must not be afraid of throwing such people together for fear it might encourage the remarriage of divorced people. On the contrary, in the Spirit of our Lord, we ought to open every possible door to a new life of happiness for these people, with the blessing of the Christian community.

The leader or leaders of such a class ought to be one of their own, not an import. A divorced or widowed teacher will usually relate better, because he has experienced the problems that are confronted by the members of his class.

From such a class can be recruited Christian evangelists who would be able to identify with the community outside the church, to minister to divorced and/or bereaved men and women who have given up on the church, with its lack of compassionate understanding.

The church should schedule regular seminars on family living and marital problems which would be open to the community at large. Whatever allocation of funds is needed should be fully arranged in view of the need. In larger churches a person could be employed, as part of the staff, to work with this group of people who have special problems. Perhaps several smaller churches could go together to provide a parish ministry of this nature, employing a coordinator in the area of caring.

Youth and adult classes would do well to invite leaders and/or members of the "singles" class to share at regular intervals the peculiar problems of being divorced or bereaved. This would promote better understanding. The pastor would do well to speak occasionally in the morning service on the church's role in divorce so as to mature and mellow the encrusted traditionalists who do much damage to a congregation.

Weddings for divorced persons should be held in the church sanctuary and open to the entire membership. To use the chapel or pastor's residence (unless particularly requested by the bride and groom) implies that the whole thing is a kind of "black market" business that should be done as quietly as possible. The total church should welcome the persons being remarried with supporting love and joy. This can do more to seal a marriage and insure its permanence than any cautious acceptance so often characteristic of church attitudes.

Special athletic opportunities are helpful. Nothing relieves tensions, relaxes nerves, and creates an atmosphere of naturalness more quickly than sports competition between church groups. A bowling team composed of singles, divorced, and widowed people might provide a common interest which could draw these people together and make them forget their loneliness for awhile. If they have a sense of humor, they might call the team "Spares and Strikes."

Local churches need to demand more from the department of practical theology in their seminaries. Entire courses dealing with divorce and/or remarriage need to be set up, courses in which future pastors and those in refresher courses can seriously confront this area of concern. Perhaps departments dealing with church and community, pastoral care, and theology could work together in creating such an in-depth course. Furthermore, similar courses need to be made available to lay persons and geared to their level of theological understanding.

No problem confronted by divorced or bereaved persons should be treated carelessly or lightly dismissed, regardless how trivial it might seem. There are no trivial troubles, except when they belong to another person. All personal needs are serious. And the needs of divorced or bereaved people are many. Every expressed need must be handled with great compassion and understanding.

Persons who have been married and are later forced to single life often complain of still feeling married. How does one face the frustration which this brings? What about the haunting inadequacy and lack of confidence in one's ability to make right decisions? How is one to go about getting back into the swing of life? What help can be found for coping with the sexual urge, which is often magnified following divorce or the death of a spouse? What can be done to conquer fear of loving again, the guilt associated with remarriage? When is it safe to accept an invitation to dinner with an available marriage partner? How can one be certain that he is not considering marriage for convenience?

There are even questions about how to handle a multitude of little things which were always cared for by the spouse who is no longer around. Some women need guidance in keeping the car in shape, help in maintaining the house, and support in a thousand and one other mundane things which they never thought about when someone else took care of them. Men sometimes need assistance in cleaning and laundry as well as cooking. If there are small children left in the care of either parent, the problems can multiply a hundredfold.

Some churches have achieved considerable success in setting up fellowship groups on an interdenominational basis, in which people victimized by the loss of a spouse can meet together. The best arrangement is that of weekly meetings, since lonely people need to be among other folk at least this often. It may be best to hold the fellowship sessions somewhere other than the local church building; some persons shy away from the church house. It frightens them with obligations which they are not ready to meet. Furthermore, there are still people who are uneasy in the edifice of another denomination. If the meetings *are* conducted within a church building, at least once a month the group could hold the fellowship at a restaurant, where they can share a nice evening around a private table.

Let us not forget how important it is to keep lonely people involved and busy. The sense of being needed is essential. Other than the usual offices of president, secretary, and treasurer, there are endless committee possibilities which provide every person with some responsibility for the entire group.

Among the committees could be publicity, public relations, church relations, legal problems, entertainment, transportation, program, athletics, telephone, crafts, literature, arrangements—the possibilities are endless.

There are also preventive measures to be taken by the church. Persons already worsted by divorce need support and understanding. But in order that fewer men and women should suffer the guilt, loneliness, and despair of marital collapse, the church must provide improved instruction for those planning to be married. Literature should be made available on a regular basis. Obviously, the selection of books, study guides, and leaflets dealing with marriage, sexual adjustment, family life, and child-rearing must be carefully made. It is not enough simply to fill a literature rack; attention should be called to the display. Furthermore, elective courses on these subjects should be offered and professional guidance ought to be provided.

When couples anticipate marriage, there should be a series of dialogue sessions with the pastor and/or a concerned lay person. Far too little time is spent together by the couple and their pastor. Sometimes there is only one counseling session, and it deals more with the particulars of the public ceremony than with understanding and establishing a new relationship. Several sessions should be set up, preferably far enough in advance of the wedding. This allows the pastor and the couple to meet weekly for six to ten weeks. These periods could deal with (1) Bible and marriage, (2) the place of sex in love and procreation, (3) divorce and remarriage, (4) children and stepchildren, (5) in-laws, (6) the management of a home, (7) relationship of the church to the newly married, etc.

Lest these periods of sharing appear to be detached from the church body as a whole, one or more couples from among the membership might share in the sessions with the pastor and counselees.

A bit of imagination coupled with an endless amount of love and understanding can turn a Christian church into a real redemption center. The church's central reason for existence is to help people find new life and hope. We are not here to perpetuate an institution or to preserve traditions. Our calling in the world is to lift the fallen and give all men and women a second chance.

To men and women worsted by the complexities of being fallen creatures living in a fallen society, the church can do nothing less than respond as does our Lord: "We do not condemn you; go, and sin no more." And we must dedicate ourselves to discovering creative means for helping them "go" and develop new lifestyles. Legalism will not have it this way at all. But love can do nothing else.

The Right
to
Marry Again

There was a period when it was my practice as a pastor to refuse *ipso facto* to solemnize a marriage in which either or both persons were divorced. By having nothing to do with the problem, I believed that my own relationship to God and my stand for his Word were above reproach. I refused to get involved. I played it safe. What did not occur to me is that non-involvement is no answer to this serious social problem. The problem of divorce is deeper than the individual sin of either or both partners. It is because of the fallenness of the human race that these symptoms of our dis-ease keep appearing. As a part of that fallen race I am involved in the hurt of mankind, whether I like it or not.

I believe now that I did not help matters by trying to "keep my skirts clean." My refusal to marry a divorced person was actually a rejection of that person's right to another chance. What is far worse, it was a refusal to acknowledge his divine forgiveness and a denial that his problem had anything to do with me.

This is not to say that a minister of the gospel should act as if divorce is not a serious matter. It is clearly a breach of the divine pattern. But so are a thousand and one other things we do as a human race. And divorce must be treated in the same manner as any of these.

How can the church justify its approach to the remarriage of divorced persons? Four basic responses normally characterize the church's attitude toward divorce and remarriage:
1) Complete repudiation and rejection of the situation as unchristian, unbiblical, and unjustifiable.

2) Willingness to accept the new marriage only if the partners are innocent and hold a legal right on the basis of the biblical exception clause.
3) Every case is welcomed for consideration. Each one is weighed on its own merits and marriage is sanctioned if there are no means of reconciliation with the former partner and the new arrangement gives promise of success.
4) Willingness to perform the marriage without serious question in light of the recognition that a marriage will be consummated anyway.

It is probably just as well that we dispense with the first and fourth of the above policies. Neither view can be defended, and therefore neither deserves serious consideration or comment. To repudiate all divorce is as unreasonably stringent as to condone all divorce is irresponsibly lenient. Such easy solutions are unworthy of the church.

The second policy listed is extremely dangerous on two points. First, it is a relaxing of the original design of God for marriage. To grant a legal loophole for skirting a clear command which affirms the indissoluability of marriage does not seem to agree with Jesus' approach to law and grace. Furthermore, as suggested earlier, there is reason to doubt the inclusion of the "exception clause" in the original manuscript of Matthew. Second, to adopt policy number two is risky business, because there is often no foolproof way of determining the innocence of one party and the guilt of the other. We have little to go on except the integrity of the person seeking remarriage. No person in a divorce case is completely innocent, since there are always ramifications unknown to anyone but God. Even when unfaithfulness is a problem, the faithful party may have been partially responsible for it.

There are three ways in which the church can justify the remarriage of divorced people. It is understood, of course, that such remarriage will be done with great care and guidance lest it be a repeat performance of the former error:

1) Recognition that the Bible does not give unambiguous instruction in the matter, and that every case has its own peculiarities which do not fit any rule. The New Testament, contrary to the opinion of more rigid legalists, is

not a law book. And it must not be treated as such. "Nowhere in the Bible is there a systematic discussion of divorce; nowhere is a clear doctrine of divorce set forth. This means that from the Biblical perspective there are many unanswered questions regarding divorce." [11]

2) All life is lived in a state of moral ambivalence. While we strive to reach perfection, we always miss it by more than inches—usually we fall short by several yards! Human relations complicate the problem, because more than one person is involved in the struggle which a husband or wife makes. "Certainly the fact of a divorce is a sign of weakness, and is an especially clear indication that we are an 'adulterous generation.' But cases are possible where not to divorce might be a sign of greater weakness, and might be a still greater offence against the Divine order." [12]

3) The church must be in the business of forgiveness. Too much judgment tends to sour people on the church. Of course, too much leniency destroys its influence as well. The balance is not easy to keep, but the church must never forget that the Christ it serves was always ready to forgive and grant a second chance. Donald Shaner puts it very well: "Where divorce is necessary for the well-being of the parties involved, it is the responsibility of the church to manifest forgiveness so that the divorced person can live purposefully within the Christian fellowship, and perhaps enter into a new, meaningful marital fellowship, a marriage so centered in Christ's love that divorce will be impossible." [13] The very purpose of the church is to assure men and women that Christ brings another chance for life and fulfilment. We must be careful not to crush the growing spirit of one whom God loves, simply because he has made a mistake.

Increasingly, pastors and other counselors are approaching the marriage of divorced people without the legalism which has obsessed us in the past. With the complexity of human problems, churchmen are usually more considerate of the persons involved than they formerly were. Clergymen are beginning to see people as more important than laws, and themselves as more than enforcers of legislation. The church is beginning to see that, although it is the earthly representative of moral and ethical truth, it is an imperfect instrument because it is made up of imperfect human beings like ourselves. "A decision must be made, but whatever it is, some wrong will be done. This is the agony for the sensitive conscience, and this is also an offence to our pride which demands the white robe of innocence. But there is no such white robe for us so long as we live in a sinful world." [14]

C. S. Lewis, in his frank way, states, "A great many people seem to think that if you are a Christian yourself you should try to make divorce difficult for everyone. I don't think that at all." [15] Much of the fault for broken marriages most likely lies in the church's failure to do a better job of counseling and guiding the marriage itself. Had the church been more concerned, perhaps we would not be so pressed by people whose marriages are on the rocks. To the degree that this is so, the church must judge itself more severely than those whom it may have failed.

The church must always sound the clear note of divine truth and judgment on sin. But we must also be as merciful and forgiving as our Lord when people suffer from their sinfulness. At the risk of spoiling its own image, the church must love the sinner and give him a chance to begin anew with the prayer that both he and the church may grow together. "Jesus always took people as he found them. None was debarred from the chance of starting again. . . . I think Jesus, while doing nothing to weaken the sanctity of marriage, would still offer the ministries of his grace in the marriage service and Holy Communion to those who 'for hardness of heart' had failed and sinned." [16]

It will be understood that these conclusions will necessitate the careful counsel and personal care so often hurried or neglected by pastors preparing for a wedding. It is necessary to learn together what created the breakdown of the marriage which has failed and to lay solid groundwork for the marriage to come. With such loving care and personal understanding, the church may better minister to the sinful both inside her ranks and outside her doors.

It is tragic that pastors are too busy to devote the time for this kind of preventative instruction. By neglecting to provide more careful counseling prior to marriage, we clergymen may be unintentionally contributing to the breakdown of marriages before they are ever consummated. For us then to act guiltless when confronted by divorced persons seeking our help in establishing a new union may be a double sin on our part.

Let it not be thought that this is a sanctioning of divorce and/or remarriage *per se*. There are some divorced persons who ought not to remarry. There is something within them which militates against the likelihood of success in any marital relationships. The church will find it unwise to offer its blessing to such an obviously hopeless union. But, by the same token, there are some single persons who give no reason for believing their marriage will work. When this is clearly apparent in the counseling sessions, the pastor should be brave enough to point it out and recommend that the couple not go through with it.

Once a marriage has been consummated, the church must love and accept the persons involved. There must be no difference in the way we treat divorced and remarried people and other persons. When there is forgiveness, there is no desire to remember the past. What is past is over.

Local Church
Guide
to Action

Developing an Action Group for Ministry:

Too much organization can be devastating to organic life within the Body of Christ. On the other hand, no body can function properly unless it is structured at least enough to delineate the responsibilities of each organ and faculty. Most churches are organized so as to care for areas of concern crucial to the local program. It would be unusual to find a church body anywhere which does not have work areas in which people plan and labor for outreach, education, and worship. To have a church without these broad divisions of ministry would be difficult, if not impossible.

Much serious thinking needs to be done about providing, within the organization of the church, opportunities for those members of the congregation who are anxious to *do* something, but are at a loss to know where to start. Every congregation would do well to have several smaller subgroups of people whose prime responsibility is ministry to special segments of the community often untouched by the typical local church. Prisoners in the community jail need regular attention. Students away at school, men and women in the armed service, minority groups, alcoholics, the bereaved, homeless and displaced persons, the retarded, the blind, and the divorced are only a few of the special needs for which action groups could be trained.

The purpose of the action group is to continue the earthly

ministry of Jesus in the interval of time between his ascension and his return to earth. Christians are the members of his body. That means that we are to be involved in alleviating the hurt of mankind, even as he was when here in the flesh. To meet these human needs requires committed, compassionate people who are willing to take the time to learn how to work with men and women who have special needs. It is not easy work. But a few people committed and organized can witness significant results if they are persistent and patient.

All this is in keeping with the mission of Jesus—to preach the gospel to the poor, to heal the brokenhearted, to preach deliverance to the captives, to make possible the recovery of sight to the blind, and to set at liberty those who are bruised (Luke 4: 18). Some people, such as these mentioned by Jesus, must be given special consideration and love. This is the purpose of the Action Group for Ministry.

Laying the Action Group Foundation

Evaluating Attitudes

1) Make a list of all the divorced people you know. How do you feel about them? What do you know of the reasons behind the divorce? How did you get your information? Is it trustworthy? Would you feel differently if you knew more? Do you think the person's personality has anything to do with your feelings about him or her? Are you prejudiced?

2) Read the following passages in the Bible which relate to divorce and write your own understanding of each: Genesis 2: 18; 24; Deuteronomy 24: 1–2; Matthew 5: 31–32; Matthew 19: 3–9; Mark 10: 2–12; Luke 16: 18; Romans 7: 1–3; 1 Corinthians 7: 1–40; Ephesians 5: 22–33. After writing your interpretation, ask yourself whether it is legalistic or in keeping with the spirit of Jesus' teaching.

3) Spend some time with the bibliography at the back of this book and choose two or three books for study. Give serious attention to the differing viewpoints asking whether you

are responding to those which agree with you and reacting against any new thought.

4) Analyze your motivation for being in the Action Group. If the motive is in any way related to your need for self-fulfilment rather than service, your ministry and effectiveness will be hampered. Is your reason for being a part of the group a burning sense of the need of others and a selfless desire to share Christ's love? Or do you have, though subtly disguised, inflated opinions about your ability to solve the world's problems? Are you paternalistic at all? Are you sure?

5) Have the entire group share together some of these personal findings. Be critical of one another in love. Point out areas of weakness. Pray together for illumination and sensitivity toward one another. Come to some general consensus at the end of the session, listing things learned together from the evaluation of attitudes.

Getting Oriented

One of the first things to be done by freshmen entering college for the first time is to get oriented. Sometimes there is an orientation assembly where these new students meet together. Or there may be a manual with specific information and guidelines to acquaint the enrollees with the campus, regulations, and government of the institution. Often something of the same routine is followed in business, military establishments, and even politics. It is absolutely compulsory that men and women understand the arena in which they will be working, the problems to be confronted, and the personnel with whom the work is to be done.

Before persons in the Action Group can get busy on the field they must size up the situation. This is done in a session or sessions in which the entire group takes an armchair look at the needs and possibilities. To be familiar with emotional and psychological needs of the divorced as well as the resources available through one's denominational headquarters is the first step in helping.

1) Investigate the world of the divorced by checking out the aids which your church can provide: films, tapes, books,

seminars, personnel, etc. Give serious consideration to every available help from the secular world as well. Most communities have access to social workers whose expertise can be invaluable. Psychiatrists, divorce lawyers, and judges are often of inestimable help in learning more about the world of the divorced.

2) There is no organization known as "Divorcees Anonymous." Therefore, persons who can help you become oriented from having experienced the problem with which you are laboring must be found wherever possible. Most persons in the Action Group will know someone divorced and/or remarried who will come and share firsthand with the persons in session. In order to facilitate this, the group should be small, warm, and free of well-known gossips. People who have been through a divorce can provide more direct help than most professionals who deal with the matter without personal experience.

3) You ought to know such important facts as the following: What percentage of the population in the area where your group will be ministering is divorced? How does this compare with the national average? Do these people come more from one economic level, ethnic group, religious body, etc? What percentage of divorcees attend church? How many broken marriages involve children? Are families of divorced persons properly cared for, so that there are no serious cases of physical or financial need? What is being done by the church, community agencies, or other organizations to meet such needs? What services are available in the community for referral of more difficult cases requiring professional assistance?

4) From a cross-section of the local church membership derive an analysis of the general tenor of the congregation toward divorce. How do church people feel about divorce? About remarriage? Is the church only a place for the sinless? Or is it a place for sinners? What about divorced people holding offices in the church? How much help can your group anticipate from the church board, the pastor, the finance committee, the committee on outreach?

Proceeding with the Actual Work of the Action Group

At the Time of the Divorce

1) In cases where the action group is able to work with these people from the time of the divorce, there is a great advantage. A representative or couple from the group would be wise to call as soon as possible after the divorce is finalized. (In situations where it is possible to work with persons during separation prior to legal divorce there is always a chance that the marriage may be saved.) This will be a period of depression for many, with great emotional strain and frayed nerves. Much compassion needs to be shown, but without leaving the impression that the victim is being pitied. In cases where there appears to be great joy in being released from a bad marriage, the group representative(s) must tread carefully. Often the grief and brokenness are delayed for these persons. When it finally comes it strikes hard. Keep in touch and be available when the reaction comes.

2) While too many words are futile at such a time, some chosen word of encouragement is always in order. If divorced persons can be spared the crushing guilt which usually accompanies marital dissolution at the beginning they will be a long way on the road to learning to live again. Since loneliness is a stimulant for oppressive guilt, concerted efforts ought to be made to keep the divorced person in circulation as much as possible. If we are to help such people, we must keep in mind that divorce often resembles death and has a similar effect to that of bereavement after a loved one has passed away. Too much solitude at these times is disastrous to one's emotional stability.

3) Immediately following a legal divorce is an excellent time to provide a good book written by one who has experienced the same thing and shares how he faced his new life (see the bibliography at the back of this book for suggestions). Some church agencies can provide, through denominational channels, cassette tapes dealing with broken marriages. Be sure that the divorced person has a copy of

the Bible handy and some kind of daily devotional guide. If you can get him into a local Bible study group the benefit will be twofold: he will derive new strength from the Word of God and he will also discover a supportive body of Christian friends.

4) Supply the addresses and phone numbers of several people who can be called on at any time. There are times when a lonely person just needs a sympathetic ear. Listening requires no formal or professional training, and it is the most productive counseling technique yet discovered. Often a prayer over the telephone can provide just the encouragement needed for going on with the business of living.

Continuing Group Work

1) One of the most pressing concerns following a divorce may be finding employment. This is particularly true for women who have not worked outside the home before. In addition to providing needed money, regular employment helps to keep a person's mind occupied and off himself. The group may have contacts which a lonely, fearful, discouraged victim of divorce may not. If not, go through the "help wanted" ads in the local newspaper with the divorced person and locate job opportunities suitable for his or her ability. You may even need to take the initiative by driving the person to the site of work for an interview.

2) Housing may be needed. At times the divorced person is suddenly without living quarters. Usually an earlier separation will have necessitated a move into an apartment or boarding room for one partner, but not always. When money is short and an ex-husband wants to help his estranged family as much as possible, finding lodging for himself which he can afford may be far from easy. In extreme cases the Salvation Army or Volunteers of America can help on a temporary basis. The YMCA is also a possibility. It may be necessary for the action group to make available, through church channels, funds sufficient to provide at least a month's lodging.

3) Don't forget the children. Where there are small children,

the problems of divorce are greatly increased. No matter how young or old the child may be, there is often damage which may not be noticed on the surface. Special attention should be given to these innocent victims until they begin to learn to adjust to being in a home with only one parent. Helping them get involved with children's or youth groups within the church can contribute to their adjustment. Steps should be taken to create an atmosphere of security for these children. They are often frightened by the changes in their lives.

4) No time should be lost in getting a community and/or church "Parents without Partners" group (these groups are called by many different names) in contact with the newly divorced. The regular meetings, sharing programs, recreation, social contacts, and communication are vitally important in keeping the divorced in the stream of life where others are overcoming similar difficulties.

Sharing within the Action Group

Great value can come to the entire group when each person or sub-group is given the opportunity to share with the whole the experiences discovered in service. It is easy for a group organized to do a specific job to become discouraged and give up because it has not been adequately informed of the good which is being accomplished through its efforts. Just as the seventy came back to Jesus after their mission, wanting to share the joy of their success (Luke 10: 17), the members of the action group will need to share their progress with each other.

Sometimes there will be happy experiences to share which will provide an inspiration for everyone. Or it may be that there will be some unhappy situations, some apparent failures which will have to be aired. These will call for much prayer and seeking after the will of God, lest they be repeated. Sometimes a group member will want advice as to how best to handle or even approach a delicate or knotty problem which he has encountered. The action group should be optimistic, remembering that this is the work of the Lord and that he is with us in every endeavor to serve in his stead. Yet, there must also be an honest recognition that not every report is going to be exciting victory. Do not make the mistake of deciding the effectiveness of the project on the basis of short-term successes.

It is not unlikely that persons who have been helpfully ministered to by group members may want to attend an action group meeting and share something of personal help. They should not be coerced into such an appearance, but the possibility of doing so should be made known. Eventually, divorced persons finding help through your group may want to become an active part of its service ministry. No better recruits could be found than those who have been through the experience and confronted with some degree of success the disciplines necessary to living again as a whole person.

Some method will need to be devised for informing the entire congregation of the work being done by the action group. Reports on the nature and function of the group may be published in the newsletter or bulletin. There may be an opportunity on "Family Sunday" to share a bit from the pulpit with the members of the church at large. The church is a family and will operate better if there is information and cooperation among the parties involved. When the congregation knows what you are doing, it can more sensibly support you and more wisely pray for your effectiveness in ministry.

The pastor himself can be greatly aided by the action group in his responsibility to minister wisely to the many kinds of people in the parish. Remember that the pastor is a busy person and should not be expected to attend your action group meetings unless a special need arises which requires his presence. It is the duty of the group to report periodically to the minister with information it has gleaned and suggestions as to how the best results can be derived from pastoral calling. Being prepared when he calls on a divorced person is of inestimable help to the pastor and creates a climate of reception which warms to his understanding and judgment.

71

How to Witness
to a
Divorced Person

In the foregoing pages we have learned several things which may now be set down as guidelines in evangelizing divorced and/or remarried persons:

Remember That. . . .

1) The divorced and/or remarried are essentially no different from anyone else. All men and women are sinners in need of the grace and mercy of God. God is no respector of persons (Eph. 6: 9). Man's salvation is neither earned by the absence of moral sin nor prohibited by the presence of it. Salvation is a free gift by which we are acquitted through faith. That is man's only solution for sin, and it works equally well for all.
2) In the sight of God there are no greater or lesser sins. Sin is a wrongness at the heart of all mankind. The symptoms—only one of which is divorce—are varied, but they all reveal the need of love and forgiveness. It is no harder for the heavenly Father to forgive adultery, divorce, or remarriage than any other transgression of the divine law.
3) Divorce and/or remarriage are not unpardonable sins. Life is not static—no one is trapped hopelessly where he is. Life goes on, and man is given a new beginning when he accepts divine forgiveness. Christ says to the person guilty of sexual sin, "Neither do I condemn thee: go, and sin no more" (John 8: 11), which means, "Now forgive yourself and get on with the business of a new life of healing and wholeness." The church can do no less.

4) There is a sense in which an honest divorce is better than a dishonest marriage. "If the inner unity of marriage has been destroyed, if love is gone, there can be no meaningful union left. What is left is only legalized cohabitation, which may be little better than legalized adultery."[18] Legalized marriage does not annul the possibility of adultery both within the contract and without.

5) Particular problems haunt people whose marriages have collapsed. Loneliness, guilt, and insecurity are always present. It is the task of the Christian witness to help alleviate these burdens by pointing to the Burden-bearer (Matt. 11: 28–30). We are never to be callous or appear helpless before these emotional problems when we have the answer in God's Word.

6) Whatever our Father has delivered us from required no less of him than the death of his Son. Our plight was as serious a matter with God as is that of the divorced and/or remarried.

Give Your Witness. . . .

The church is called to be God's agent in redeeming the divorced. We are not to toss these people aside on the scrap heap. God loves them and wants them for himself. If we treat such persons with pharisaical callousness, our judgment will be greater than theirs. The church complains because so many doors are closed to it in many areas of today's world. But there is a vast mission field in the millions of lost, lonely people all around us who have been worsted by divorce. Let us look no further, but get on with the work of compassionate redemption—burying our legalistic attitudes once and for all.

1. On the basis of what Christ has done for you, just share his love. Let that love be seen in your acceptance of the person who is divorced. Leave theological concerns alone. Details of doctrine are of no consideration when sharing Christ.

2. If you are a divorced Christian, you may share your freedom in Christ from a personal perspective. If not divorced, do not presume to know how the divorced person feels.

3. With love and compassion for a person made in God's image, for whom Christ died, breathe forgiveness in every word—as Christ himself would do.
4. In gratitude for God's mercy to you as one who was as hopeless as any divorced person until Christ accepted you, let your radiant thankfulness be seen.
5. Remember that witnessing is not limited to what you say. Take time to listen to the other person. Ask helpful questions, but do not overlook the questions in the heart of the one with whom you are sharing your Lord. Admit that you do not have *all* the answers, but let your confident assurance be evidenced in that you are positive anyone can find *the* Answer in commitment to Jesus Christ as Savior and Lord.

Some Helpful Books on the Art of Witnessing

Anderson, Ken. *A Coward's Guide to Witnessing*. Carol Stream, IL: Creation House, 1972.

Kennedy, D. James. *Evangelism Explosion*. Wheaton, IL: Tyndale House.

Little, Paul. *How to Give Away Your Faith*. Downer's Grove, IL: Inter-varsity Press, 1966.

Peace, Richard. *Witness, Witness, Witness*. Grand Rapids, MI: Zondervan Publishing House, 1971.

Rinker, Rosalind. *You Can Witness with Confidence*. Grand Rapids, MI: Zondervan Publishing House.

Scarborough, L. R. *How Jesus Won Men*. Grand Rapids, MI: Baker Book House, 1972.

Notes

1. Dale Galloway, *Dream a New Dream* (Wheaton, IL: Tyndale House, 1975), p. 8.

2. C. S. Lewis, *Christian Behavior* (New York: Macmillan, 1944), p. 30.

3. Karl Barth, *On Marriage* (Philadelphia: Fortress Press, 1968), p. 40.

4. Guy Duty, *Divorce and Remarriage* (Minneapolis: Bethany Fellowship, 1967), p. 130.

5. Carl F. H. Henry, *Christian Personal Ethics* (Grand Rapids, MI: Eerdman's, 1957), p. 312.

6. W. R. Inge, *Christian Ethics and Modern Principles* (London: Putnam's Sons, 1930), p. 390.

7. Albert Knudson, *The Principles of Christian Ethics* (New York: Abingdon, 1943) p. 208.

8. Norman Geisler, *Ethics: Alternatives and Issues* (Grand Rapids, MI: Zondervan, 1971), p. 205.

9. Paul Ramsey, *Basic Christian Ethics* (New York: Scribner's, 1952), p. 74.

10. T. B. Matson, *The Christian, the Church, and Contemporary Problems* (Waco, TX: Word Books, 1968), p. 101.

11. Ibid., p. 101.

12. Emil Brunner, *The Divine Imperative* (Philadelphia: Westminister Press, 1947), p. 362.

13. Donald Shaner, *A Christian View of Divorce* (Leiden: E. J. Brill, 1969), p. 109.

14. David H. C. Read, *Christian Ethics* (Philadelphia: Lippincott, 1969), p. 118.

15. Lewis, *Christian Behavior*, p. 35.

16. Alan Walker, *How Jesus Helped People* (New York: Abingdon, 1974), p. 26.

17. Louis Cassels, *The Real Jesus* (New York: Doubleday, 1968), p. 79.

18. Matson, *The Christian, the Church, and Contemporary Problems*, p. 105.

Bibliography

Bainton, Roland H. *What Christianity Says About Sex, Love, and Marriage*. New York: Association Press, 1957.

Easily-read summary of the church's attitudes toward marriage from New Testament times to the present day. Written briefly in layman's style.

Barth, Karl. *On Marriage*. Philadelphia: Fortress Press, 1968.

Entire book is a superb analysis of divinely ordained marriage as monogamous and permanent. Chapter 5 is particularly significant in regards to the church's role in the remarriage of divorced persons.

Brunner, Emil. *The Divine Imperative*. Philadelphia: Westminster Press, 1947.

A basic theological understanding of Christian ethics as surveyed a quarter of a century ago. Pages 359–367 present a view of divorce and its results which still speaks authoritatively today.

Cassels, Louis. *The Real Jesus*. New York: Doubleday, 1968.

Of limited value except that it is by a modern newspaperman who expresses the feeling of the common people about the problem. See pages 76–79.

Duty, Guy. *Divorce and Remarriage*. Minneapolis: Bethany Fellowship, 1967.

Written from a purely legal, biblical viewpoint in which the author makes an excellent case for the right to divorce and remarriage in instances of porneia, or anti-Christian rejection of a Christian mate.

Galloway, Dale E. *Dream a New Dream*. Wheaton, IL: Tyndale House, 1975.

The autobiographical account of how a clergyman confronted his own divorce and the emotional problems resulting from it.

Geisler, Norman. *Ethics: Alternatives and Issues.* Grand Rapids, MI: Zondervan, 1971.

The chapter on sex is especially helpful.

Goode, William J. *After Divorce.* Glencoe, IL: Free Press, 1956.

An extensive survey of divorced people taken to determine reasons for divorce, complications, adjustments, and remarriage problems.

Harkness, Georgia. *The Sources of Western Morality.* Grand Rapids, MI: Eerdman's, 1957.

Brief section on marriage and divorce is rather generalized and adds little that is new.

Henry, Carl F. H. *Christian Personal Ethics.* Grand Rapids, MI: Eerdman's, 1957.

Ponderous work. Extremely valuable conservative contribution. Statements on divorce are so scattered as to require use of index. Voluminous documentation helpful. Book useful to understand evangelical-conservative approach.

Inge, W. R. *Christian Ethics and Modern Problems.* London: Putnam's Sons, 1930.

While somewhat old, the book has something to say from the liberal slant of the period.

Knudson, Albert. *The Principles of Christian Ethics.* New York: Abingdon, 1943.

Philosophical treatment of the whole generalized area of ethics. Short but helpful approach to divorce issue on pages 205–207.

Lewis, C. S. *Christian Behavior.* New York: Macmillan, 1944.

Chapter 6 on "Christian Marriage" offers some pungent observations about the performance of marriage, meaning of love, and distinctions between civil and ecclesiastical marriage.

Lovett, C. S. *The Compassionate Side of Divorce.* Old Tappan, NJ: Fleming H. Revell, 1975.

A more flexible look at divorce from a known conservative writer. Good insights.

Maston, T.B. *The Christian, the Church, and Contemporary Problems.* Waco, TX: Word Books, 1968.

Chapters 7 and 8 provide a sane and logical analysis of the changing culture and its influence on the home. A good study in the church's difficult stance on divorce and remarriage.

O'Neill, William L. *Divorce in the Progressive Era.* New Haven: Yale University Press, 1967.

Superb history and analysis of the developing concept of divorce and remarriage from 1880 to 1919—called "The Progressive Era."

Peterson, J. Allen, ed. *The Marriage Affair.* Wheaton, IL: Tyndale House, 1971.

Limited in help for divorced persons, but generally helpful in understanding the relationship of marriage.

Ramsey, Paul. *Basic Christian Ethics.* New York: Scribner's, 1952.

Limited but enlightening section on meaning of biblical material and interpretation in modern world. Several brief notations which must be found in index.

Read, David H. C. *Christian Ethics.* Philadelphia: Lippincott, 1969.

Entire book deals with the underlying Christian ethic and offers valuable suggestions for dealing with difficult issues. Chapter 8 is particularly helpful on the ambivalence built into divorce and war.

Saul, Leon. *Fidelity and Infidelity.* New York: Lippincott, 1967.

A popular treatment of reasons for marital breakup by a physician concerned with the hereditary and environmental forces that shape persons. Especially pages 211–214 on "Divorce and the Choice of a Mate."

Shaner, Donald W. *A Christian View of Divorce*. Leiden: E.J. Brill, 1969.

Excellent study of the biblical, historical, and theological framework in which marriage is to be viewed. Also a good summary of modern church responses.

Stewart, Suzanne. *Divorced!* Grand Rapids, MI: Zondervan, 1974.

The story of a divorced mother of three who confronts the gigantic problems of keeping a home with God as her only support.

Thielicke, Helmut, *The Ethics of Sex*. New York: Harper, 1964.

Penetrating insight into the issues revolving around the order of marriage in Section III. Particular help with the church's place in divorce on pages 104–125, 182–192.

Walker, Alan. *How Jesus Helped People*. New York: Abingdon, 1974.

Chapter 2 is an approach to divorce and remarriage by a compassionate, contemporary pastor in Australia. Being a realistic clerical struggle with an age-old problem, the approach throws needed light on the relationship between truth and love.